I would like to thank Apostle Prude for the opportunity and honor to write the foreword for his book. I was introduced to Apostle Prude through my spiritual father the Late Dr. Apostle Clifford E. Turner approximately 20 years ago. Apostle Prude is one of God's generals, a true apostle, a prophet and a mentor. I've known him to operate in the gifts of healings, miracles and give an accurate word of prophecy. Anointed as a father in the gospel, he's a revelatory teacher of the Word of God. His insight into the Word has allowed him to be a blessing to me and my family with wisdom and a sure word of the Lord.

As an African-American male married to a Caucasian woman of 33 years, I have firsthand experience with the stigma surrounding interracial marriage discussed in this book as well as the mental anguish society places on an African-American male who marries outside of his race. I didn't give my best in my marriage not understanding my identity and God's purpose, feeling as though my life wasn't approved or ordained by God. If a book of this caliber had been available 30 years ago, I could have avoided many misconceptions and mistakes. I'm so appreciative to Apostle Prude's sensitivity to this delicate subject as he educates and empowers with the Truth from God's Word.

Apostle Terrence A. Malone

This book is phenomenal, the more I read the more excited I got! It is scripturally based, with sound doctrine according to God's plan. Being in an interracial marriage not everyone approves still today in 2019, however I am not in this marriage for the approval of man but for Kingdom Purpose. My husband and I were the first interracial couple to be married by Apostle Joseph Prude on July 9, 2016, All of the Brides side was white, and all of the Grooms side was Black. Apostle Joseph Prude stood in Awe and said with the condition of America today, our marriage was about Kingdom purpose.

Johnny and Susan Cummings

Absolutely Superb! Eye opening. The biblical research and the revelation of God's view of interracial marriages has been made plan. Recommend reading for the body of Christ.

Larry and Kathy James

Interracial Marriage

Chief Apostle Joseph Prude

Scripture quotations are from:

The Holy Bible, King James Version, Holman Christian Standard Bible, and the American Standard Version

Visit the author's website at: www.AJP Ministries.com

All rights reserved. No part of this book may be reproduced or transmitted in any form or by any means without written permission of the author

Contents

Chapter 1	Interracial Marriage	1
Chapter 2	The Origin of Race/ The Origin of What is Called the Races	3
Chapter 3	The First Interracial Marriage Recorded in the Scriptures	8
Chapter 4	What is God's Purpose in Race Mixing?	10
Chapter 5	More Interracial Marriage	13
Chapter 6	A Mixed Marriage that Never Happened	16
Chapter 7	Judah	22
Chapter 8	Joseph	23
Chapter 9	Four Hundred Years Later	25
Chapter 10	Casualties of Racism	26
Chapter 11	There is No Light in Them	30
Chapter 12	False Teachings	39
Chapter 13	Historical Data on Interracial Marriage	43
Chapter 14	Indian and Black Interracial Marriage	50

Chapter 15	The World is Sometimes Ahead of the Church	52
Chapter 16	Dake's 30 Reasons for Racial Separation	55
Chapter 17	The Color of the Ancient Egyptians	58
Chapter 18	What is the Devils Purpose in His Opposition to Interracial Marriages	60
Chapter 19	Interracial Marriage the Solution to America's Racial Problem	65
Chapter 20	A Coat of Many Colors	71
Chapter 21	More Scriptural Examples of Interracial Marriage in the Scriptures	75
Notes		79
Book Ordering Information		81

CHAPTER ONE

INTERRACIAL MARRIAGE

Romans 2:11 "For there is no respect of persons with God." I believe that Interracial marriage is certainly an issue the church needs to address head on. There are many topics of interest the church seems to avoid; interracial marriage is one of them. So often, the people of God find themselves unable to relate to many issues of importance, and that is because they are without clear scriptural understanding on these particular matters.

We function as if we not only, do not have a God, but also as if we do not have His great written Word. Scripture has a voice on just about everything. God has definitely weighed in with a great deal of commentary, as it pertains to racial mixing and marriage between the races. When the Holy Spirit birthed the idea of this book in my spirit, I asked the Lord in prayer, "What is Your purpose that I write this book?" His answer led me to this scriptural verse:

II Corinthians 10:5 (KJV)

"Casting down imaginations and every high thing that exalteth itself against the knowledge of God and bringing into captivity every thought to the obedience of Christ."

If you will take a look at II Corinthians 10:4, you will see that the Word instructs us in "...pulling down strongholds." In actuality, the entire area around race and interracial marriage is a stronghold of the devil.

This tool in the hand of the devil has served as nothing less than a weapon of destruction against the purposes of God. Saints, we desperately need to apply God's Word to every area of our lives. We do not need the opinion of man with regard to race, culture or religious preference, we simply need the Word. As some of you may well know, there even exists a "so-called fundamental, bible believing college," that has brought tremendous reproach to the body of Christ due to their purporting a doctrine of racial separation that is most assuredly unscriptural. I pray that this book will serve to bring light to you and break down any demonic strongholds you may need to see defeated in this area.

CHAPTER TWO

THE ORIGIN OF RACE/ THE ORIGIN OF WHAT IS CALLED THE RACES

Genesis 9:18-19: "And the sons of Noah that went forth of the ark were Shem and Ham and Japheth and Ham is father of Canaan. These are the three sons of Noah, and of them was the whole earth overspread."

In this verse of scripture, we find listed, post-flood, the names of Noah's three sons, and they are Shem, Ham, and Japheth. From Noah's three sons come three basic racial groups.

White, Black, and Brown. All other people groups are a mixture of the original three. I want to encourage you to take a moment and read Genesis 10. In doing so, you will notice that the descendants of Noah's sons and their tribes, migrated throughout the whole earth.

Genesis 10 (KJV)

1. Now these *are* the generations of the sons of Noah, Shem, Ham, and Japheth: and unto them were sons born after the flood.
2. The sons of Japheth; Gomer, and Magog, and Madai, and Javan, and Tubal, and Meshech, and Tiras.

3 And the sons of Gomer; Ashkenaz, and Riphath, and Togarmah.
4 And the sons of Javan; Elishah, and Tarshish, Kittim, and Dodanim.
5 By these were the isles of the Gentiles divided in their lands; everyone after his tongue, after their families, in their nations.
6 And the sons of Ham; Cush, and Mizraim, and Phut, and Canaan.
7 And the sons of Cush; Seba, and Havilah, and Sabtah, and Raamah, and Sabtecha: and the sonsof Raamah; Sheba, and Dedan.
8 And Cush begat Nimrod: he began to be a mighty one in the earth.
9 He was a mighty hunter before the **Lord**: wherefore it is said, Even as Nimrod the mighty hunterbefore the **Lord**.
10 And the beginning of his kingdom was Babel, and Erech, and Accad, and Calneh, in the land of Shinar.
11 Out of that land went forth Asshur, and builded Nineveh, and the city Rehoboth, and Calah,
12 And Resen between Nineveh and Calah: the same *is* a great city.
13 And Mizraim begat Ludim, and Anamim, and Lehabim, and Naphtuhim,
14 And Pathrusim, and Casluhim, (out of whom came Philistim,) and Caphtorim.
15 And Canaan begat Sidon his firstborn, and Heth,
16 And the Jebusite, and the Amorite, and the Girgasite, 17 And the Hivite, and the Arkite, and the Sinite,
18 And the Arvadite, and the Zemarite, and the Hamathite: and afterward were the families of the Canaanites spread abroad.
19 And the border of the Canaanites was from Sidon, as thou comest to Gerar, unto Gaza; as thou goest, unto Sodom, and Gomorrah, and Admah, and Zeboim, even unto Lasha. 20 These *are* the sons of Ham, after their families, after their tongues, in their countries, *and* in their nations.

21 Unto Shem also, the father of all the children of Eber, the brother of Japheth the elder, even to him were *children* born.
22 The children of Shem; Elam, and Asshur, and Arphaxad, and Lud, and Aram.
23 And the children of Aram; Uz, and Hul, and Gether, and Mash.
24 And Arphaxad begat Salah; and Salah begat Eber.
25 And unto Eber were born two sons: the name of one *was* Peleg; for in his days was the earthdivided; and his brother's name *was* Joktan.
26 And Joktan begat Almodad, and Sheleph, and Hazarmaveth, and Jerah,
27 And Hadoram, and Uzal, and Diklah,
28 And Obal, and Abimael, and Sheba,
29 And Ophir, and Havilah, and Jobab: all these *were* the sons of Joktan.
30 And their dwelling was from Mesha, as thou goest unto Sephar a mount of the east.
31 These *are* the sons of Shem, after their families, after their tongues, in their lands, after their nations.
32 These *are* the families of the sons of Noah, after their generations, in their nations: and by these were the nations divided in the earth after the flood.

Let's take a moment to hone in on some key facts. You will notice, in verse 8, that Cush, the son of Ham who begat Nimrod, who became the first great leader after the flood, was the creator of Babel, which later became known as Babylon. It is important to note that Nimrod being a descendant of Ham was black. I want you to note the importance of this verse and clearly see this, so that we may begin to understand that God has both blessed and used all people. Remember, we are pulling down strongholds.

One of the worst strongholds ever, is this notion that blacks have never done anything of value. Well, Scripture certainly pulls down this lie. In Genesis 10:18 we want to also make note of the fact that the Canaanites and their families were spread abroad. In other words, this black tribe migrated across the entire earth. It is very simple to understand that when people migrate, it is only natural that they assimilate with the people that they have migrated among. It is here, that we witness the beginning of what is referred to as "race mixing" in Scripture. It is ironic that this information should be found in the book of Genesis. The word Genesis means beginning and the beginning of all things is found in the book of Genesis.

In verses 2-5, of Genesis 10, we see the descendants of Japheth. These are the Caucasian people, their tribal tongues, and nations. Some of the tribal names like Comer, Magog, Tubal, and Meshech are the tribes that inhabited the area that is known today as Russia and Eastern Europe. Mascouche is the root word from which the word Moscow is derived. Moscow is the capital of Russia. Tarshish is the area which is known as modern Spain. So from the lineage of Japheth we see the origins of the Caucasian people.

As we look into verses 21-31 we see the descendants of Shem. From Shem come the Semitic peoples. This people group inhabited the area of northern Africa and the Middle Eastern regions. These people are also referred to as an "oriental people." Abraham was descended from the lineage of Shem, which means the physical head of Israel was a Semite. As you continue further in Scripture, you will see how the racial make-up of the Hebrew people began to change. For further clarity, we will take a look at the meaning of the names of Noah's sons:

- The name Japheth - means expansion
- The name Ham - means hot, black or dark
- The name Shem - means renown, conspicuous or authority

Genesis 11:2 (KJV) "And it came to pass, as they journeyed from the east, that they found a plain in the land of Shinar; and they dwelt there."

The inhabitants of the earth began a migration east, from the direction of Eden, until they they came to the land of Shinar, in which they settled. From this scripture it is pretty clear that all of known mankind, at this time, were together as a people group, because at this point they still had one language. In verse 6 of this chapter, when the Lord came down, He said, "Behold the people is one." The word 'one' is the Hebrew word (echad), which means united or altogether alike. This means there existed no racial divisions. Now, when the Lord scattered them abroad, it was the Lord who confounded their language and the confounded language served as the basis for their scattering.

So, the separation of people, in the mind of God, was done based on confounded language and not based on a difference in race. We have yet to see Scripture prove out that people were divided by race, and race has never been in the mind of God as a reason for division. Tribes and tongues is what has divided people. As a matter of fact, it is division that even exists within racial groups, therefore bringing about different subgroups. For example, it is a known fact that different Indian tribal groups speak different languages, but at the end of the day they are all still Indians.

CHAPTER THREE

THE FIRST INTERRACIAL MARRIAGE RECORDED IN THE SCRIPTURES

Genesis 16:3 "And Sarai Abrams wife took Hagar her maid the Egyptian after Abram had dwelt ten years in the land of Canaan and gave her to her husband Abraham to be his wife."

We read in this passage of scripture that Sarai has given Hagar, her maid, as a wife to Abram, because Sari could not have children. Hagar was an Egyptian. Remember, the Egyptians are descendants of Ham, but Abram was a Semite. From this union came what is known as the Arabs. The Arabs are a Mixture of Hametic and Semitic people. Thus, we see the first interracial marriage in Scripture. From this union came Ishmael, Abraham's first son, the son of a mixed marriage. Show me in Scripture God's pronouncements against this marriage! There are none. Does this surprise you? Well, it should not. God has never been against interracial marriage. Racial separation has always been the devil's idea, never God's.

In Genesis 16:10 (KJV), we read, "And the angel of the LORD said unto her, I will multiply thy seed exceedingly, that it shall not be numbered for multitude."

Interracial Marriage

Here we have the Lord speaking in the form of the Angel of the Lord. Hagar is given a promise that her seed will multiply exceedingly. We can clearly see God's blessing on the seed of this union. The Lord was apparently pleased with this union. This was shown forth in His promise to bless the offspring of this union and multiply them exceedingly.

I believe this promise goes even further. I believe it was also a promise to multiply the children and offspring of this mixed marriage, all the way through history, until this very day. If you will take a closer look at the statistics throughout the world, you will see there exists over 250 million Arabs. We have in the world, 33 million African-Americans. African-Americans are very much the product of racial mixing; two thirds of African Americans have at least one white ancestor. One third of all African-Americans has Indian ancestry. South America, particularly Brazil, is a continent of mixed people. The people of South America are a composition of racial groups. For the most part they refer to themselves by national names rather than racial.

It would almost be an impossibility, anyhow, because there actually exists no racial tag that would fit. Brazil is a nation of over 100 million people. Brazil is a melting pot blend of every racial group mixture known as Brazilian. I believe in my spirit that this is the future of America. The inhabitants of the Pacific Islands, of Hawaii, as well as the Samoan Islands are very much part African in their features. These people are also part Indian and part Caucasian. God has truly blessed the offspring of mixed unions and multiplied them greatly. I believe this has always been His purpose.

CHAPTER FOUR

What is God's Purpose in Race Mixing?

Genesis 1:26 (KJV) "And God said, Let us make man in our image, after our likeness: and let them have dominion over the fish of the sea, and over the fowl of the air, and over the cattle, and over all the earth, and over every creeping thing that creepeth upon the earth."

When God created man he created man in His image. By design, man is to be the vehicle through which God expresses Himself. If you will notice in this verse, the Godhead talks among themselves and says let us make man in our image. This shows us the plurality of God and the multiple personalities of the Godhead. The different traits and attributes being expressed through each member of the Godhead, God the Father, God the Son, and God the Holy Spirit. In the first man, all that God is, in His entirety, could not possibly be expressed through one type of man. God had to create an infinite variety of character and composition in man, in order to have the means by which He could express His limitless personality.

This is why He started with Adam and then down through Noah and his sons. God made all men of one blood. It is very much like a snowflake, all snowflakes are made from the same material... water, but they are limitless in their variety. All snowflakes also reflect light differently because of the variation

Interracial Marriage

in their form, but not one snowflake is MORE than another. Likewise, each racial group seems to have built into it some unique ability to express the nature of God. Blacks react to the Holy Spirit differently than whites, but it is still the same Spirit. If you attend different worship services in which the composition of the congregation is predominantly black or predominantly white, you will in most cases find two different kinds of worship styles, but God is in both forms. "Praise God!"

This gives the Holy Spirit a broader spectrum by which to express more of who God is. In other ways we see God taking character traits and mixing them to bring about new traits. Racial mixing is the ongoing process of creation. God creates new people from old people. It is very simply seen when we mix two different paint colors and come up with a new color. In the mind of God, this new color, which is the composition of two or even three colors, always existed, but would have never been known by man until God did the mixing.

Genesis 1:28, (KJV), "And God blessed them, and God said unto them be fruitful and multiply and replenish the earth." The word multiply is the Hebrew word (rabah) which means to increase, bring up, enlarge etc. It was God's purpose that men would expand and enlarge. How was this to come about? Well, when you multiply, you add to what is already there, you make it more than what it was originally.

When you multiply you take a number of the value of two, (2), or greater and multiply it with another number that is different than the original but having components of each number blended into the new number. I have been amazed when I have viewed pictures of African-Americans of the early 1900's. The one thing that impressed me most, in every picture, was how much darker black folks were in those pictures and in those times. There has certainly been a gradual change. This is due largely to mixing.

CHAPTER FIVE

MORE INTERRACIAL MARRIAGE

Genesis 26:34-35 (KJV)

"And Esau was forty years old when he took to wife Judith the daughter of Beeri the Hittite, and Bashemath the daughter of Elon the Hittite: 35 which were a grief of mind unto Isaac and to Rebekah."

The Hittites were descendants of Heth. Heth was a Canaanite. We already know that the Canaanites were descendants of Ham from which the black tribes came. If we look back at Genesis 10:15, (KJV), we read, "And Canaan begat Sidon, his firstborn, and Heth." Now we see Esau, who is a Semite, has married two wives and both of them are black descendants of Ham. I think it is important to make note of the grief and concern of Esau's parents. The concern was not that their child chose to marry a person of another race, but the fact that the child married someone outside of their spiritual beliefs.

What makes this even more amazing is the fact that Isaac already had a half-brother in Ishmael, a brother who was born of Hagar, a black woman. This makes Isaac and Rebeckah's attitude even more amazing. But thanks be to God, in that He never hides anything, it all comes out on the pages of the Bible.

THE MIXTURE GOES ON

Genesis 36:1-3 (KJV), "Now these are the generations of Esau who is Edom, Esau took his wives of the daughters of Canaan, Adah the daughter of Elon the Hittie and Aholibamah the daughter of Anah the daughter of Zibeon the Hivite; and Bashemath Ishamael's daughter, sister of Nebajoth."

We see here that God has mixed the melting pot even more. Not only has Esau married two black wives, Adah and Ajolibamah, but he has also married a third wife, Bashemath, Ishamael's daughter, sister of Nebajoth." Now we have to remember that the Hivites were descendants of Ham, as we have read in Genesis 10:15-17. Esau's third wife also comes from the descendants of Ham.

MORE ON ABRAHAM'S LINE

I think it is most noteworthy to again see the mixture in the descendants of Abraham. Let's take a look at Genesis 30: 3-4.

3   And she said, Behold my maid Bilhah, go in unto her; and she shall bear upon my knees, that I may also have children by her.
4   And she gave him Bilhah her handmaid to wife: and Jacob went in unto her.

The Bible tells us that Rachel, Jacob's wife, is unable to have children. She tells Jacob to go into her maid Bilhah. Jacob goes in unto Bilhah and she bares Jacob a son. This firstborn son is named Dan. Bilhah, again bares a son, and the second son's name is Naphtali. These are two of the twelve tribes of Israel. Next, Leah, Jacob's other wife, did the same thing, which we read in verse 9-13:

⁹ When Leah saw that she had left bearing, she took Zilpah her maid, and gave her Jacob to wife.
¹⁰ And Zilpah Leah's maid bare Jacob a son.
¹¹ And Leah said, A troop cometh: and she called his name Gad.
¹² And Zilpah Leah's maid bare Jacob a second son.
¹³ And Leah said, Happy am I, for the daughters will call me blessed: and she called his name Asher

Now we see that Leah gave Jacob her maid Zilpah, and Zilpah bares two sons, one is named Gad and the other son is named Asher. This now adds two more tribes in Israel. I believe this makes it even more clear that racial purity is some misguided notion from the devil. We have no proof that these two women, Bilhah and Zilpah, were Hebrews or Semitic. If we follow the biblical pattern we know that Sarah's maid was an Egyptian. So, we can extrapolate from this that more than likely Bilhah and Ziplah are of another race outside of Hebrew or Semitic.

CHAPTER SIX

A Mixed Marriage that Never Happened

Read Genesis 34:1-31

1. And Dinah the daughter of Leah, which she bare unto Jacob, went out to see the daughters of the land.
2. And when Shechem the son of Hamor the Hivite, prince of the country, saw her, he took her, and lay with her, and defiled her.
3. And his soul clave unto Dinah the daughter of Jacob, and he loved the damsel, and spake kindly unto the damsel.
4. And Shechem spake unto his father Hamor, saying, Get me this damsel to wife.
5. And Jacob heard that he had defiled Dinah his daughter: now his sons were with his cattle in the field: and Jacob held his peace until they were come.
6. And Hamor the father of Shechem went out unto Jacob to commune with him.
7. And the sons of Jacob came out of the field when they heard *it*: and the men were grieved, and they were very wroth, because he had wrought folly in Israel in lying with Jacob's daughter; which thing ought not to be done.
8. And Hamor communed with them, saying, The soul of my son Shechem longeth for your daughter: I pray you give her him to wife.
9. And make ye marriages with us, *and* give your daughters unto us, and take our daughters unto you.

10 And ye shall dwell with us: and the land shall be before you; dwell and trade ye therein, and get you possessions therein.
11 And Shechem said unto her father and unto her brethren, Let me find grace in your eyes, and what ye shall say unto me I will give.
12 Ask me never so much dowry and gift, and I will give according as ye shall say unto me: but give me the damsel to wife.
13 And the sons of Jacob answered Shechem and Hamor his father deceitfully, and said, because he had defiled Dinah their sister:
14 And they said unto them, We cannot do this thing, to give our sister to one that is uncircumcised; for that *were* a reproach unto us:
15 But in this will we consent unto you: If ye will be as we *be*, that every male of you be circumcised;
16 Then will we give our daughters unto you, and we will take your daughters to us, and we will dwell with you, and we will become one people.
17 But if ye will not hearken unto us, to be circumcised; then will we take our daughter, and we will be gone.
18 And their words pleased Hamor, and Shechem Hamor's son.
19 And the young man deferred not to do the thing, because he had delight in Jacob's daughter: and he *was* more honourable than all the house of his father.
20 And Hamor and Shechem his son came unto the gate of their city, and communed with the men of their city, saying, 21 These men *are* peaceable with us; therefore let them dwell in the land, and trade therein; for the land, behold, *it is* large enough for them; let us take their daughters to us for wives, and let us give them our daughters.
22 Only herein will the men consent unto us for to dwell with us, to be one people, if every male among us be circumcised, as they *are* circumcised.

23 *Shall* not their cattle and their substance and every beast of theirs *be* ours? only let us consent unto them, and they will dwell with us.

24 And unto Hamor and unto Shechem his son hearkened all that went out of the gate of his city; and every male was circumcised, all that went out of the gate of his city.

25 And it came to pass on the third day, when they were sore, that two of the sons of Jacob, Simeon and Levi, Dinah's brethren, took each man his sword, and came upon the city boldly, and slew all the males.

26 And they slew Hamor and Shechem his son with the edge of the sword, and took Dinah out of Shechem's house, and went out.

27 The sons of Jacob came upon the slain, and spoiled the city, because they had defiled their sister.

28 They took their sheep, and their oxen, and their asses, and that which *was* in the city, and that which *was* in the field, 29 And all their wealth, and all their little ones, and their wives took they captive, and spoiled even all that *was* in the house.

30 And Jacob said to Simeon and Levi, Ye have troubled me to make me to stink among the inhabitants of the land, among the Canaanites and the Perizzites: and I *being* few in number, they shall gather themselves together against me, and slay me; and I shall be destroyed, I and my house.

31 And they said, Should he deal with our sister as with an harlot?

In this story Shechem the son of Hamor the Hivite, had a sexual encounter with Dinah, the daughter of Leah. Now the Hivites were, again, the descendants of Ham. We can bear this out from our Scripture reference in Genesis 10:6-16. This means Shecham was a descendant of Ham and the Hamitic people were black people. Now Dinah was a Semite a descendant of Shem. Now after Shechem had a sexual relationship with Dinah he loved her. He now asks his father Hamor to get her for his bride. When Hamor met with

Jacob, to discuss this matter, we see no objection from Jacob based on race. Jacobs's sons were angry because of what had transpired sexually. In verse 9 Hamor said:

Genesis 34:8-9, (KJV), "And Hamor communed with them, saying, The soul of my son Shechem longeth for your daughter: I pray you give her him to wife. 9 And make ye marriages with us, and give your daughters unto us, and take our daughters unto you."

Hamor requested of Jacob that all of their sons and daughters intermarry. Notice we see no racial prohibition to these unions, God did not talk to Jacob in a dream, neither did an Angel. There was no message to Jacob that this should not be done. The only reason these marriage relationships did not happen is because the sons of Jacob were angry at the sexual defilement of their sister Dinah, but not because of the race of Shechem or their religious differences.

Genesis 34:14 (KJV) "14 And they said unto them, We cannot do this thing, to give our sister to one that is uncircumcised; for that were a reproach unto us:"

Jacob was all too willing to agree to these marriages between his sons and daughters and the daughters of Hamor the Hivite. The thing to notice in this story is that these two people of different races thought it perfectly natural to mix and intermarry. There was never any mention or concern about the racial difference, this was not the issue.

My prayer is that as you read these truths from the scripture, that the Holy Spirit will begin to bring down any strongholds of tradition that may be housed within your mind and that the eyes of your understanding will be open so that you may increase in the knowledge of Him. The burden of my heart is that this teaching will give light to the church. The Bible says, "... that every valley be filled and every mountain and hill be made low, that the crooked way be made straight and that the rough way be made smooth." (Luke 3:5, not verbatim)

PROPHECY

Thus saith the Lord, "My People, I would speak unto you to receive these words, that I may open your eyes unto the truths hidden in the scriptures. My people, My word is the final authority on all things. I will begin in this hour to bring down the lies and deceit of the devil. Many of My people have refused to stand up for the truth. But I send this word unto you to bring insight and revelation. This is the hour wherein you shall behold many wondrous things from My word. Many people have been damaged by the lies of the devil. It has been My purpose to bring all people together freely. Satan has been the one who has desired to separate people by race. I would cry out unto you, be still and know that I am God.

Be still in your hearts and minds and I will begin to tear down every wall that has been erected by the devil. My people I will raise up voices in the land that will not fear to speak My word and My counsel. My servants have avoided these words. They have allowed the true seed of the word of God to be mixed with other seed. The vine of truth has not been pure, but I will raise up a pure word. The world has watched as My people have shunned the depths of truth of My word.

The world has watched as they have sought for answers to the issues of life. But My people, the ones who are the oracles of God, have not come forth with the truth. I say unto you, My people, spare not, but cry aloud and show My people, their transgressions and the house of Jacob their sins.

For it was My plan to bring people of every race together. Yet many times My purpose has been perverted as the devil has convinced you that it was not designed to bring together people of all races. I will now speak to you about this area; this shall be a word that will not go away for I will send forth this word. It will be given from every direction. I will raise up voices to speak on every issue of this life. I will raise up warriors of My word that will cry out and speak with boldness, says God. The Lord would say this word, yet their are some who will not receive this word, but reject it, and call it the flesh. This is just the beginning of what I will speak in this hour, let Me circumcise the foreskins of your hearts."

CHAPTER SEVEN
....

JUDAH

Genesis 38:1-2 "And it came to pass at that time, that Judah went down from his brethren, and turned into a certain Adullamite, whose name was Hirah. And Judah saw their daughter of a certain Canaanite whose name was Shuah and he took her and went in unto her."

What we have here, is yet another scriptural encounter with regard to racial mixing and interracial marriage. Judah is one of the sons of Jacob, Judah was the first born of Jacob. Judah marries a Canaanite woman, (Black Women), so again we see interracial marriage. Interracial marriage has always been part of the plan of God. If you read the rest of this story, we later discover that Judah engages in sex with his own daughter -in-law, Tamar. She conceives and had twin sons from her father-in-law. She named the first born son Pharez and the second son, Zerah. If you take a look at the genealogy of Jesus in Matthew, Chapter 1, you will see that Jesus, Himself, was descended through this line, He was of the tribe of Judah. Jesus' lineage, according to the scripture, can be traced back to Judah through Pharez, the son of Judah's daughter-in -law. The point being, that all the ideas and concepts about racial purity and bloodlines, that run rampant, do not really carry any weight, nor have much value, when they are compared to the scriptural revelation of what really happened in God's dealing with man.

CHAPTER EIGHT

JOSEPH

THE TRIBES OF EPHRAIM AND MANASSEH

Genesis 41:45 "And pharaoh called Joseph's name Zaphnathpaaneah and he gave him to wife Asenath, the daughter of Potipherah, the priest to On. And Joseph went out over all the land of Egypt."

Joseph was taken down into Egypt and sold into slavery by his own brothers, because of their jealousy. After working in Potiphar's house, after prison and much affliction, God then exalts Joseph to become Pharaoh's right-hand man. Pharaoh gives Joseph the daughter of Potiphar, the priest of On, as his wife. From this union came two sons.

Genesis 41:50-52, (KJV), "And unto Joseph were born two sons before the years of famine came, which Asenath the daughter of Potipherah priest of On bare unto him. And Joseph called the name of the firstborn Manasseh: For God, said he, hath made me forget all my toil, and my father's entire house. And the name of the second called he Ephraim: For God hath caused me to be fruitful in the land of my affliction."

So again, we have interracial marriage. The offspring of this marriage became two of the tribes of Israel. Joseph being one of the twelve patriarchs of Israel, and his descendants were these children born of interracial marriage. To see their inclusion in Israel, we will read Numbers 1:10.

Numbers 1:10, (KJV), "Of the children of Joseph: of Ephraim; Elishama the son of Ammihud: of Manasseh; Gamaliel the son of Pedahzur."

Lord God, that we would see the truths of these scriptures. God, Himself, is the great Chef of the melting pot. He is the one that in His great wisdom, mixed in the different ingredients of humanity.

CHAPTER NINE
Four Hundred Years Later

We now see the children of Israel having multiplied abundantly, until the land was filled with them. God had greatly blessed them as He had promised. It would be safe to assume that when the 66 children of Israel first entered Egypt, with the compliments of Pharaoh, they quickly began to marry the Egyptians because their brother Joseph had already set the precedent by his marriage to the daughter of an Egyptian priest. 400 years later we see Israel fleeing Egypt with 600,000 men, plus women and children. In Exodus 12:37-38 we get a glimpse of what this Exodus group of people looked like.

Exodus 12:37-38, (KJV), "And the children of Israel journeyed from Rameses to Succoth, about six hundred thousand on foot that were men beside children, and a mixed multitude went up also with them and flocks."

CHAPTER TEN

Casualties of Racism

Romans 12:2, (KJV)

And be ye not conformed to this world. But be ye transformed by the renewing of your mind, that ye may prove what is that good and acceptable and perfect will of God."

One day the Lord spoke a word to me as I was in meditation, and this is what He said, "There are people that do not exist today. Some people may never exist, yet they will only exist in the mind of God."

In other words, there are people that will never live. People that God purposed to live, but the devil blocked their would be existence, through racism. I tell you, when the Lord spoke this to me, it overwhelmed me. Every single person that has ever walked across the face of planet earth, existed first in the mind of God, first in the realm of eternity. Then there are the others, the people that will never actually live out a life on planet earth.

Notice what the Lord told Jeremiah in Jeremiah 1:5, (KJV), "Before I formed thee in the belly I knew thee...." The word knew here is the Hebrew word (Yada), which means 'to observe and to know by seeing.' In other words, before Jeremiah was actually birthed into existence on planet earth, God already spoke him as a fact in eternity.

There is not one single person on the face of the earth that is accidental and without purpose.

Psalms 139:14-17, (KJV), says, "I will praise Thee, for I am fearfully and wonderfully made; marvelous are Thy works, and that my soul knoweth right well. My substance was not hid from Thee when I was made in secret, and intricately wrought in the lowest parts of the earth. Thine eyes did see my substance, yet being imperfect; and in Thy book all my members were written, which in continuance were fashioned, when as yet there were none of them. How precious also are Thy thoughts unto me, O God! How great is the sum of them!" David, under a prophetic anointing, stated that every person that will ever live, preexisted in the mind of God. Verse 15 says, "My substance was not hid from you when I was made in secret." The word substance (or the word Ostem), means body; in other words, God knew David's racial composition before he was even born. The verse goes on to say, "Your eyes did see my substance...." The word substance, as we have said, is body, the word see, used here, is the word (Raah) which speaks of prophetic visions, to look ahead; to see supernaturally. This means that God actually sees our body long before we are put into it. He further states, in verse 16, "How precious also are thy thoughts unto me, O God how great is the sum of them." The concept seems inconceivable, yet true; you already existed in God's thoughts. He thought about you in the dateless past.

To now bring this line of thought into focus, let us consider this; everything that is purposed by God does not necessarily happen. The fact of the matter is, is that man has his part to play in his need to cooperate with God. Just as God told Israel, in Jeremiah 29:11, (KJV), "For I know the thoughts that I think towards you, saith the Lord, thoughts of peace and not of evil, to give you an expected end." The Lord had many wonderful thoughts and purposes for Israel that never happened. They existed in the spirit, but never took place in the natural. Why? Because the devil was able to maneuver Israel out of the place of blessing by their rebellion and sin so that they never realized God's highest and His best. They saw the permissive will of God, but they failed to experience His perfect. This now brings us to the discussion of marriages. This will include revelation and insight that the Lord has shared with me.

God has dealt with me for many years, as He has revealed to me that there are many marriages that He ordained to be, but were interracial. These marriages never happened, because the devil was able to thwart their manifestation through his stronghold of resistance to interracial marriage in the earth. Through some of these 'would-be-unions,' there were people to be born, people with a God-deposit inside of them for such a time as this. These people will never be. The devil has been able to prevent their birth, by preventing the marriages of their parents.

Just as abortion has aborted many doctors, scientists, statesmen, preachers, etc., so has the stronghold against interracial marriage, prevented many doctors, lawyers, scientists, etc., from ever coming into existence. We have allowed racism to prevent the birth of many great vessels of God. Interracial marriage brought forth the tribes of Ephraim and Manasseh. My question is, how can they possibly be viewed as an accident?

Perhaps we may not be found guiltless if we have allowed the cure for cancer to linger in the mind of God, only. It may very well be, that the vessel that God planned to use to bring the cure into the world, was to be the product of a mixed marriage. If the devil had succeeded in preventing mixed marriages, in the genealogy of Jesus, Jesus would never have been born. I think of some of God's great servants of this hour, Morris Cerullo, the product of Jewish and Italian linage. I think of Barack Obama, the son of an Irish woman and a black African. I think of the evangelist, Tim Storey, the son of a mixed marriage. I think of the musician, Israel Hougthon, again, the son of a mixed relationship. When we get to heaven and stand before God, I wonder if we will be given the chance to visit the hall of fame of those that never were?

CHAPTER ELVEN

THERE IS NO LIGHT IN THEM

Isaiah 8:20

To the law and to the testimony: if they speak not according to this word, it is because there is no light in them.

Let us consider another area to be addressed on our subject matter. The vast number of published bible commentaries, with margin notes, that contain actual commentary of many of these Bible Scholars and teachers. It is important to realize one significant fact; these writers are still mere men. It does not matter who they make themselves out to be. If what they say tends toward racism, separation and/or fear, then we must conclude that God is certainly not speaking through them on this subject matter.

As I researched this subject, I found that just about every Bible commentator that I read gave a "justifiably" different reason why Moses' Cushite wife could not have possibly been a black woman. I went through many battles in my own mind. I said, "Lord, these are great men, men of renown, that have written these bible notes and commentaries." I was at the point I literally felt faint as I listened to their endless rhetoric!

When I researched the marriage of Joseph, even to Pharaoh's daughter, it was still the same kind of stonewalling and racially biased explanations.

Most of the commentary purposed to avoid the mention of who these ancient Egyptian people actually were, racially.

If you desire to see the absolute plain truth, with regard to this matter, and have the plain truth deposited within your spirit, you may have to set some of your bible commentaries and margin notes to the side, because these commentaries are simply not going to speak to the truth on these issues.

Miriam and Aaron spoke against Moses—It appears that their jealousy over the power and influence he possessed was the real cause of their complaint, albeit his marriage to an Ethiopian woman- השאה תישכה haishshah haccushith— THAT WOMAN, the Cushite, probably meaning Zipporah, who was an Arab, born in the land of Midian, was the ostensible cause.

A COMMENTARY AND CRITICAL NOTE: ADAM CLARKE

"Moses married a Midianite, a daughter of the priest of Midian (Ex. 2:15-25; 3:1; 4:18-26; 18:1-27; Num. 10:29-36; Judg. 1:16; 4:11; 1 Sam. 15:6). The land of Midian in Arabia was the land of Cush as well as Ethiopia because one branch of Cush settled there in ancient times. Midian was a son of Abraham through Keturah (Gen. 25:1-4). Therefore, Moses married a descendant of the son of Abraham, not an African as some think. She was simply a Cushite because she dwelt in the land of Cush, in the same sense that a German or an Italian immigrant becomes an American because of citizenship.

Just as being American has no reference to race, so being a Cushite did not identify Zipporah in this way. Some say she was a second wife of Moses, but we have no grounds for this supposition." (**Dake's Annotated Reference Bible: Containing the Old and New Testaments of the Authorized or King James Version Text.**)

NOTES FOR VERSE 1 (MIRIAM, AARON & MOSES)

1. Verse 1. An Ethiopian woman -- Hebrew, "a Cushite woman" -- Arabia was usually called in Scripture the land of Cush, its inhabitants being descendants of that son of Ham (see on Exodus 2:15) and being accounted generally a vile and contemptible race (see on Amos 9:7). The occasion of this seditious outbreak on the part of Miriam and Aaron against Moses was the great change made in the government by the adoption of the seventy rulers [Numbers 11:16]. Their irritating disparagement of his wife (who, in all probability, was Zipporah [Exodus 2:21], and not a second wife he had recently married) arose from jealousy of the relatives, through whose influence the innovation had been first made (Exodus 18:13-26), while they were overlooked or neglected. Miriam is mentioned before Aaron as being the chief instigator and leader of the sedition. (**Dake's Annotated Reference Bible: Containing the Old and New Testaments of the Authorized or King James Version Text.**)

Interracial Marriage

NOTES FOR VERSE 2
(MOSES' MARRIAGE TO
ZIPPORAH - THE ETHIOPIAN)

1. Zipporah, who is here called an Ethiopian, in the Hebrew a Cushite, because she was a Midianite: the word Cush being generally used in scripture, not for Ethiopia properly so called below Egypt, but for Arabia. If she be meant, probably they did not quarrel with him for marrying her, because that was done long since, but for being swayed by her and her relations, by whom they might think he was persuaded to chose seventy rulers, by which co-partnership in government they thought their authority and reputation diminished. And because they durst not accuse God, they charge Moses, his instrument, as the manner of men is. **(Dake's Annotated Reference Bible: Containing the Old and New Testaments of the Authorized or King James Version Text.)**

a. Some other woman, whom he married either whilst Zipporah lived, or rather because she was now dead, though that, as many other things, be not recorded. For, as the quarrel seems to be about his marrying a stranger, it is probable it was a fresh occasion about which they contended. And it was lawful for him as well as any other to marry an Ethiopian or Arabian woman, provided she were, a sincere proselyte. **(Dake's Annotated Reference Bible: Containing the Old and New Testaments of the Authorized or King James Version Text.)**

b. It is interesting to note that in every case each Bible expository had a different reason, and different explanation as to why Moses' Cushite wife was not an African. I can accept this line of logic and reasoning, if the logic remains consistent continually, as it relates to the Scriptures and to other references as it pertains to Cushite in the Scriptures. Only in the case of Moses' Cushite wife, do the Bible expositors somehow explain that they suddenly discovered a whole new group of Cushites who were not African, but according to their explanation, they were in fact Arabs. I will prove this point by showing you some other examples in the Scriptures where we have the word Cushite used, in these cases Bible expositors have no disagreement, whatsoever, with the fact that this was a black African, particularly when they were found in some area of servitude.

Let's look at some examples:

THE ETHIOPIAN EUNUCH

Jeremiah 38:6-13, (KJV)

"Then took they Jeremiah, and cast him into the dungeon of Malchiah the son of Hammelech, that was in the court of the prison: and they let down Jeremiah with cords. And in the dungeon there was no water, but mire: so Jeremiah sunk in the mire. 7 Now when Ebedmelech the Ethiopian, one of the eunuchs which was in the king's house, heard that they had put Jeremiah in the dungeon; the king then sitting in the gate of Benjamin; 8 Ebedmelech went forth out of the king's house, and spake to the king, saying, 9 My lord the king, these men have done evil in all that they have done to Jeremiah the prophet, whom they have cast into the dungeon; and he is like to die for hunger in the place where he is: for there is no more bread in the city. 10 Then the king commanded Ebedmelech the Ethiopian, saying, Take from hence thirty men with thee, and take up Jeremiah the prophet out of the dungeon, before he die. 11 So Ebedmelech took the men with him, and went into the house of the king under the treasury, and took thence old cast clouts and old rotten rags, and let them down by cords into the dungeon to Jeremiah. 12 And Ebedmelech the Ethiopian said unto Jeremiah, Put now these old cast clouts and rotten rags under thine armholes under the cords. And Jeremiah did so. 13 So they drew up Jeremiah with cords, and took him up out of the dungeon: and Jeremiah remained in the court of the prison."

This is a most familiar story to just about everyone who is a student of the Bible. It speaks of the great prophet Jeremiah's deliverance from out of a dungeon, after the King had ordered him to be placed there. I found it of rather peculiar interest, as I studied this passage of Scripture, that none of the Bible expositors found it necessary to explain away who this particular Ethiopian happened to be. This, however, is in stark contrast to what I previously showed to you about the comments of the Bible expositors commentary on an Ethiopian.

Again, the Hebrew word Cush or Cushite, in this case, was frequently translated Ethiopian. So the expositors were more than willing to accept that this particular man was a Nubian or one that came from Abyssinia. The word Abyssinia is a word used interchangeably for Ethiopia. The expositors seemed to find no need to invent new Ethiopians or Cushites for this passage.

Ebed-melech -- The Hebrew designation given this Ethiopian, meaning "king's servant." Historically, even at this early juncture, God desired to show what good reason there was for calling the Gentiles to salvation. An Ethiopian stranger is the one who saves the prophet, whom his own countrymen, the Jews, tried to destroy. Therefore, the Gentiles believed in Christ, whom the Jews crucified, and the Ethiopians were among some of the earliest converts (Acts 2:10, 41 Acts 8:27-39). Ebed-melech, was most likely the keeper of the royal harem, and so he therefore had private access to the king. The eunuchs over harems in this present day are mostly from Nubia or Abyssinia.

NOTES FOR VERSE 8

A Commentary: Critical, Experimental, and Practical on the Old and New Testaments.

If the Ethiopians were indeed not black Africans, then why would the Holy Spirit inspire the writer to reference the color of the skin of the Ethiopians in the following verse:

Jeremiah 13:23, (KJV), "Can the Ethiopian change his skin, or the leopard his spots? Then may ye also do good, that are accustomed to do evil."

Here again, it is very plain to see from scriptural study, that due to the bias of Eurocentric biblical commentators, we find ourselves faced 'head-on' with the constant opposition to interracial marriage in societies in which we live. This bias is certainly demonic, in it's origins, and it surfaced via Eurocentric Bible commentators. This book has been written in order to help cast down, pull down, uproot and destroy this rampant spirit of racism.

Philippians 4:9

Those things, which ye have both learned, and received, and heard and seen in me, do. Imitation is a natural and spiritual principle. I am sure, just as the people of Israel admired Moses, we can be certain that many also followed his example.

Moses' marriage helped to bring down racial barriers. If the people of God, at the very least, do not have their minds and hearts right about issues of racial bias, then who will? We must be the city situated high on a hill, casting a bright light on these dark issues. We must be the place where the world can come and discover the revelation light and insight concerning all things. It is a shame when the church thinks like the world, when we refuse to function with God's mind with regard to the issues of this life. To show you just how important the church's stance on race really is, let me share with you something that the Lord shared with me. The Lord spoke this following word to me:

"Son, if the church had taken the right stand about slavery, there would have never been a Civil War."

Let me explain this and also give you some history. The origins of the white Southern Baptists convention was birthed out of their support of slavery. They were at one point, the Southern Baptists, part of a larger Baptist convention that was nation-wide. It turned out that the Southerners, in the convention, refused to repudiate slavery. As a matter of fact, they actually gave tacit approval of it. In most every case, they vigorously supported slavery. Due to their position, they ultimately left the larger Baptist convention, and started the old convention called the Southern Baptists, which was built on their support of slavery. These Southern Baptists were the ones that had the opportunity to speak into the spirits and hearts of the people in the south, with regard to this issue, but they abdicated their prophetic responsibility. So in turn, it was God who had to judge the south for the position they had taken on slavery, and unfortunately, the judgment of slavery came via the Civil War. The brunt of the ravages of the Civil War were levied against the south, because of the judgment of God, and this resulted in the south's lost of the Civil War. Please understand, this is true church history, so even if it makes you angry, it is still the truth.

A WORD OF ADVICE

Proverbs 18:22, (KJV)

Whoso findeth a wife findeth a good thing, and obtaineth favour of the LORD.

If God has lead you to fall in love with a person of another race, praise God for it, and feel free go forth in faith. My hope is that the words of this book will set you free from any concerns that you may have had previously. To think that somehow God is against interracial marriage, with God being no respecter of persons is totally erroneous. As a matter of fact, it is quite the contrary, it is actually part and parcel of one of God's great plans. If any spirit tells you anything else, it is not of God. It is, in fact, the spirit of error which teaches doctrines of devils.

CHAPTER TWELVE

False Teachings

II Timothy 2:15 "Study to shew thyself approved unto God, a workman that needeth not to be ashamed, rightly dividing the word of truth." Over the years there have been certain scriptural references, that many have used, in order to justify their need to teach against interracial marriage. This tactic has caused some to believe these false teachings are seemingly, backed by scriptures. It has also lead others to believe that racial separation is divine.

We will, by the light of the Holy Spirit, take a clear look at some of these passages, in order that we may better determine what God actually has to say on this matter.

I Kings 11:1-8

"But King Solomon loved many foreign women, together with the daughter of Pharaoh: women of the Moabites, Ammonites, Edomites, Sidonians, and Hittites—2 from the nations concerning which the Lord said unto the children of Israel, "Ye shall not go in to them, neither shall they come in unto you, for surely they will turn away your heart after their gods." Solomon cleaved unto these in love. 3 And he had seven hundred wives, princesses, and three hundred concubines; and his wives turned away his heart.

4 For it came to pass, when Solomon was old, that his wives turned away his heart after other gods; and his heart was not perfect with the Lord his God, as was the heart of David his father. 5 For Solomon went after Ashtoreth the goddess of the Sidonians, and after Milcom the abomination of the Ammonites. 6 And Solomon did evil in the sight of the Lord, and went not fully after the Lord, as did David his father. 7 Then Solomon built a high place for Chemosh the abomination of Moab, on the hill that is before Jerusalem, and for Molech the abomination of the children of Ammon. 8 And likewise did he for all his foreign wives, who burned incense and sacrificed unto their gods." In just a casual reading of the previous passage, you will quickly be able to see certain truths:

1. The Lord was not concerned about the race, but the nation. There is a difference between a race and a nation. For example, all U.S. citizens are Americans, but "American" does not define their race. Races of people have certain physical characteristics that are peculiar to them, and it stops there, while nations have certain cultural and religious and political characteristics that are peculiar to them. This was even more so, during the time that this passage was written. God was concerned about the mixing of bloodlines and the mixing of bloodlines changes nothing but physical attributes. The greater danger for Israel was the national practices of the Mobaites, Ammonites, Ecomites, Zidonians and Hittes. Notice in verse two "for surely they will turn your heart after their Gods."

2. Notice the verse did not say, "they will turn your skin another color." Races of people do not have their own gods. The national practices of these people, with all their different types of Idolatrous worship, this is what God did not want

Interracial Marriage

Israel to marry into! It is the same way today, God does want believers to be unequally yoked with unbelievers, race means nothing. If you find a good mate white, black, yellow or brown; you have found a good thing. We also do not want to fail to remember that pIsrael was already a mixed people by this time. If you have read this book, the Bible, you have seen the mixed racial composition of Israel.

It would be most hypocritical of God, after He has orchestrated the racial mixing of Israel, to now tell Her that this was never His purpose or plan. God's issue with Solomon's marriage to Pharaoh's daughter was strictly because of the religious beliefs of Egypt, beliefs from which she was not yet converted. So the entire issue was never the race of these women, but their religions.

Deuteronomy 7:2-3, (KJV), "And when the LORD thy God shall deliver them before thee; thou shalt smite them, and utterly destroy them; thou shalt make no covenant with them, nor shew mercy unto them: 3 Neither shalt thou make marriages with them; thy daughter thou shalt not give unto his son, nor his daughter shalt thou take unto thy son."

These are the words spoken by Moses. Now let's keep in mind that Moses had already married a black Cushite woman, and he was also raised by a black family. Do not forget, it was God that stood for Moses in the vindication of Moses' marriage.

Moses could not possibly tell the people, after being in a racially mixed marriage, himself, that now Jehovah forbade it. What the Lord did not want, again, is for the people to take on the practices of the nations around them. God was concerned about the people of Israel being turned away from Him, because of their immoral way of life. The foul sexual practices of the temple prostitutes, as well as the homosexuality they practiced, was all part and parcel of their wicked idolatrous worship.

So again, there is no scriptural basis that is in opposition of people of different races being married. At the end of the day, racial mixing has actually always been the plan and purpose of God.

CHAPTER THIRTEEN

HISTORICAL DATA ON INTERRACIAL MARRIAGE

Ecclesiastes 1:9-10

"The thing that hath been, it is that which shall be; and that which is done, is that which shall be done; and there is no new thing under the sun. Is there anything whereof it may be said, "See, this is new?" It hath been already in olden times which were before us."

Hopefully, we have clearly proven to you that interracial marriage is scriptural. The biblical record shows us one example after another, of races intermarrying. There is also a very large body of far more information that speaks to the history and facts with regard to 'race mixing,' down through the years. For instance, in the United States, the ratio stands that 3 out of every 4 Black Americans has at least one white ancestor. Four fifths, (4/5), of all American Indians claim other races in their bloodlines, versus the notion of pure Indian blood.

- Famous historian H.G. Wells said, "Everyone alive is, I am convinced of mixed ancestry. But some of us are more white, some of us more black, and some of us more Chinese."
- In South Africa, a fourth of the people classified as white have non-white ancestors.

- Two-thirds of Americans, who list their ancestry as English, also list other ancestral influence.
- Only 45% of the American population is without any other race in there backgrounds.
- In a review of the records of family 'coats of arms,' in European countries, over 497 of the 'coats of arms' revealed That there were blacks in the family line.
- From 1890 until 1910, 600,000 blacks disappeared, based on their decision to pass for white.
- There was a time, in the nation of Brazil, that Brazil actually sold off certificates of whiteness. Due to racial intermarriage, however, whites ceased to exist in Brazil, as a distinct racial group.
- In Boston, interracial marriage topped out at a high of 13.6% of all black marriages in 1900-1904, it dropped to 5.2% in 1914 -1918, and even lower at 3.7% in 1934-1938.
- In 1967 the Supreme Court struck down laws that banned mixed marriages. Since that time there has been a 92.3% increase in interracial marriages.

The statistics reveal that from 1970-1977 it was 13% for black males-white females; 25% increase for black female-white males. In 1977 there were 95,000 black males married to white women and 20,000 black females married to white men.

- In 1985 there were 164,00 black and white married couples and 47,000 black women married to white men.
- In the Ohio Journal of Science, Robert P. Shucker, of the Ohio State University; Department of Sociology reported that of 21% of all American whites, 1 out of 5

have African ancestors. Twenty-Eight million whites are descendants of persons of African ancestry.
- For Blacks, statistics show that 70 to 80% have white or Indian ancestors.
- Recorded data published in The Anthropometry of the American Negro by Melvin J. Herskovits, in 1930, reveals 71.7% of blacks had white ancestors, 27.2% had Indian ancestry.

Only 22% of black Americans were of unmixed African blood. -In the state of Virginia, in 1959, a white man and his black wife were convicted by an all-white jury for violating the state's ban on interracial marriages.

- **How many new marriages are interracial today?**
  The number of interracial marriages has increased 5 times since 1967. Today, approximately 17% of married couples are interracial.
- **How many couples that are still married today are interracial?**
  1 out of 10 every married people, or 11 million people, are married to someone of a different race than themselves.
- **What percentage of African Americans marry someone of a different race?**
  18 % of African Americans marry someone of a different race. This is 13% higher than in 1980, when only 5% of African Americans married someone from a different race.
- **What percentage of whites marry someone of a different race?**
  11 % of white people marry someone of a different race today, compared to 4% in 1980.

- **What percentage of Asians marry someone of a different race?**
  People of Asian descent are the most likely to marry someone from a different race, as 29% of Asians today marry outside their ethnicity.
- **What percentage of Hispanics marry someone of a different race?**
  Hispanics come in second as the most likely to marry outside their ethnicity. 27% of Hispanics today are married to someone outside their race.
- **What is the most common racial pairing today among newlywed couples?**
  Today, the most common interracial pairing is one Hispanic spouse and one white spouse. This combination makes up 42% of interracial marriages today.
- **Which state has the highest number of interracial newlyweds?**
  Hawaii has the largest number of interracial newlyweds today. 42% of newlyweds in Honolulu are mixed race. The next city with the largest number of interracial marriages is Las Vegas, with 31% of married couples being interracial.
- **When did the ban on interracial marriage end?**
  The ban on interracial marriage ended with the decision of Loving vs Virginia on June 2, 1967.
- **What percentage of recently married black men have a spouse of a different race?**
  African American men have a higher likelihood of marrying outside their race. Men marry someone of another race 24% of the time.

Interracial Marriage

- **What percentage of recently married black women have a spouse of a different race?**
  African American women are less likely to marry outside of their race. Women marry someone of another race approximately 12% of the time.
- **What percentage of nonblack adults oppose a relative marrying a black person today?**
  Today's society is much more accepting of interracial marriage. Just a little more than 25 years ago, 63% of nonblack adults opposed interracial marriage. Today, that number is only 14%.
- **What percentage of people with just a high school diploma marry someone from a different race?**
  14 % of people with just a high school diploma and no college marry outside of their race.
- **What percentage of people with a college degree marry someone from a different race?**
  19 % of people with a bachelor's degree marry someone from a race other than their own.

MISCELLANEOUS FACTS

- **How many infants today are biracial?**
  Today, 14% of infants are biracial. This is 9% higher than the 5% of biracial infants in 1980.
- **What percentage of the population is biracial?**
  According to a study conducted by Pew Research, 6.9% of the adult population is biracial. This is slightly elevated from the estimate provide by the Census Bureau, but the study takes into account the heritage of each adult, not just their self-reported race.

- **What is the racial breakdown of the U.S. population?**
  As of the latest census, the racial breakdown in the U.S. is as follows:
    - White: 76.9%
    - African American: 13.3%
    - American Indian: 1.3%
    - Asian: 5.7%
    - Native Hawaiian: 0.2%
    - More than 2 races: 2.6%
- **What percent of interracial couples end up in divorce?**
  Approximately 41% of mixed-race couples end up in divorce within the first 10 years of marriage.
- **What percent of same-race couples end up in divorce?**
  Approximately 31% of same-race couples end up in divorce after 10 years.
- **Who was the first interracial couple?**
  Mildred and Richard Loving were the first white man and African American woman to marry despite the law against interracial marriage. As a result, they both spent time in jail and were forced from their home state of Virginia, seeking refuge in Washington.
- **What is Loving Day?**
  Loving Day is celebrated on June 12th every year and signifies the day the Supreme Court overruled the ban on interracial marriage.
- **How long were the Lovings married?**
  The Lovings were married for 17 years before Richard was tragically killed in a car accident in 1975.

JUDGES OPINION

"Almighty God created the races: white, black, yellow, and red and placed them on separate continents. If it were not for your interference with this arrangement there would be no cause for such marriages. The fact that he separated the races, shows that he did not intend for the races to mix."

CHAPTER FOURTEEN

INDIAN AND BLACK INTERRACIAL MARRIAGE

There has been a tremendous level of interracial marriage among American Indians and blacks which dates as far back as the pre-Columbus visits of Blacks from West Africa. There was a continual racial mixing, even during the colonial era and also, during the time of slavery, as slaves ran away and lived among Indian tribes. In a survey of 1,551 black Americans, one third, (1/3), of them claimed to have Indian blood. There are several Indian tribes that ceased to exist as Indians, as a result of the massive inflow of black African blood. Many of the southern Indian tribes, which were located in the southeastern part of this country, became havens of rescue for the slaves that fled from slavery.

In the 1780's, certain white Virginians began to agitate for the termination of the Gingaskin Indian Reservation in Northampton County. In 1812 it was argued that as many black men, as Indians, now inhabited the place. The Indian women have married many black men, and a majority of the inhabitants are blacks or have black-blood in them. The real Indians are few. The reserve was divided, (allotted), in 1813 and by 1832 whites had acquired most of it.

In the state of Tennessee, the Melungen Indians mixed freely with blacks, and in 1834 they were declared black. The Seminole Indians, of Florida, are another black

Indian tribe. There is hardly a Seminole Indian, that exists today, that does not have black blood in his veins.

"There has never been a taboo from God against interracial marriage." I want to say this again, as it rises up in my spirit,

"There has never been a taboo from God against interracial marriage." The Lord is very displeased with the chorus of silence from the church in this area. The Gospel is the light of God, to the entire world, on every subject. Proverbs 28:5 says, "Evil men understand not judgment: but they that seek the Lord understand all things." Many times, while in the process of writing this book, the enemy attacked my mind and said this subject violates, it is not the gospel and it is without value. But the Holy Spirit said to me time and time again, that these words will bring healing to My people, and that these words will bring to mind the purposes of God. So we give you these truths as a labor of love and to set you free in your thinking.

CHAPTER FIFTHTEEN
....

THE WORLD IS SOMETIMES AHEAD OF THE CHURCH

Luke 16:8 "For the children of this world are in their generation wiser than the children of light."

Of recent, there has been a large number of Hollywood movies, dealing with the subject matter of interracial relationships. In almost every case, the films were done on the basis of the current value system of the world, as it pertains to race, as a dominant theme. In almost every instance, in which sexual themes were depicted, it only served to add flames to an already smoldering fire.

The world has tied into the storylines of these movies, it's own ideology of how to address what they perceive as a social issue that is in desperate need of social change. Meanwhile the church, who has God-given power and authority to speak out on these matters, runs and hides. This is not good! Where is the church? She is conspicuously silent.

It is very, very sad! How many times will God have to allow the world to bring forth the light that He has equipped the church to be responsible to bring forth? In 1990 there were 200,000 new black and white marriages in the U.S., or 4 out of every 1000 married couples, were interracial. In 1975, 1.5 % of every 1000 married couples were black and white marriages. This is a change that we will continue to see increase in our nation. Praise God for it!

There is certainly a far more open forum in the world, by which we are able to bring truth in this area, than what we find in the church at this time. Maybe the church, in the mind's of some, is the place where truth is what you selectively want it to be. I believe if we are going to understand the gospel of the Kingdom, we must understand what Jesus preached, Jesus preached the Word!

Mark 2:2, (KJV), "And straightway many were gathered together, insomuch that there was no room to receive them, no, not so much as about the door: and he preached the word unto them."

The word, "Word," means the Logos in the Greek. The word logos means the divine expression. In other words, God expressed His mind on any and every subject that exists. Believe this, The Lord has something to say about every subject, and it is not just "Praise the Lord, Hallelujah, Praise the Lord!" He has a certain mindset as it pertains to all subject matter. Oh, that we would allow God to bring His wisdom through us, and to this world! This is a world that is groping for answers to the complex problems of this hour.

In 1967 the Supreme Court struck down laws against mixed marriages, and might I also add, that this was in the face of strident opposition from some parts of the church world. Since that time, there has been a 92.3% increase in interracial marriage, which 131% is for black males- white females, this data is from a survey done in 1970-1977.

In 1985 there were 164,000 black-white married couples added to this group. (Even today in the year 2012 white evangelical Christians are more opposed to interracial marriage than any other group in America according to a recent survey done by the Pew Research Foundation. Even today 16% of white evangelical Christians say that interracial marriage is bad for society. This is a higher percentage than even what the people of the world say...what a shame. When will the church become the light of the world that we have been called to be? My hope is that this book, in some small way, contributes to a breakthrough in this area.

PROPHETIC WORD

The Lord says, "My people, the house of the living God is filled with the doctrines of men. I call for a pruning of your minds and your hearts. For My ways are not your ways, neither are your thoughts My thoughts. I will bring your mind into line with My mind, if you will allow Me to do so. This is the hour when the church shall be a beacon of light, and the city sitting upon a hill. A light that is brightly shining with divine truth of God, as it relates to the issues of the hour. I will cause the world to come to the church, even with the questions of this life. My church shall be unpolluted and undefiled with the doctrines of their own minds, but shall be conduits for this truth of God."

CHAPTER SIXTEEN

Dake's 30 Reasons for Racial Separation

1. God wills all races to be as He made them. Any violation of God's original purpose manifests insubordination to Him (Acts 17:26; Romans 9:19-24)
2. God made everything to reproduce "After his own kind" (Genesis 1:11-12, 21-25; 6:20; 7:14). Kind means type and color or He would have kept them all alike to begin with.
3. God originally determined the bounds of the habitations of nations (Acts 17:26; Genesis 10:5, 32; 11:8; Deuteronomy 32:8)
4. Miscegenation means the mixture of races, especially the black and white races, or those of outstanding type or color. The Bible even goes farther than opposing this. It is against different branches of the same stock intermarrying such as Jews marrying other descendants of Abraham (Ezra 9-10; Nehemiah 9-13; Jeremiah 50:37; Ezekiel 30:5).
5. Abraham forbad Eliezer to take a wife for Isaac of Canaanites (Genesis 24:1-4). God was so pleased with this that He directed whom to get (Genesis 24:7, 12-27).
6. Isaac forbad Jacob to take a wife of the Canaanites (Genesis 27:46-28:7).
7. Abraham sent all his sons of the concubines, and even of his second

wife, far away from Isaac so their descendants would not mix (Genesis 25:1-6)
8. Esau disobeying this law brought the final break between him and his father after lifelong companionship with him (Genesis 25:28; 26:34-35, 27:46; 28:8-9).
9. The two branches of Isaac remained segregated forever (Genesis 30; 46:8-26).
10. Ishmael and Isaac's descendants remained segregated forever (Genesis 25:12-23; 1Chronicles 1:29)
11. Jacob's sons destroyed a whole city to maintain segregation (Genesis 34)
12. God forbad intermarriage between Israel and all other nations (Exodus 34:12-16; Deuteronomy 7:5-6)
13. Joshua forbad the same thing on sentence of death (Joshua 22:12-13)
14. God cursed angels for leaving their own "first estate" and "their own habitation" to marry the daughters of men (Genesis 6:1-4; 2 Peter 2:4; Jude 6-7)
15. Miscegenation caused Israel to be cursed (Judges 3:6-7; Numbers 25:1-8)
16. This was Solomon's sin (I Kings 11)
17. This was the sin of Jews returning from Babylon (Ezra 9:1-10:2,10-18,44; 13:1-30)
18. God commanded Israel to be segregated (Leviticus 20:24; Numbers 23:9; 1 Kings 8:53)
19. Jews recognized as a separate people in all ages because of Gods choice and command (Matthew 10:6; John 1:11). Equal rights in the gospel gives no right to break this eternal law.
20. Segregation between Jews and all other nations to remain in all eternity (Isaiah 2:2-4; Ezekiel 37; 47:13-48,55; Zechariah 14:16-21; Matthew 19:28; Luke 1:32-33; Revelation 7:1-8; 14:1-5)

21. All nations will remain segregated from one another in their own parts of the earth forever (Acts 17:26; Genesis 10:5,32; 11:8-9; Deuteronomy 32:8; Daniel 7:13-14; Zechariah 14; Revelation 11:15; 21:24)
22. Certain people in Israel were not even to worship with others (Deuteronomy 23:1-5; Ezra 10:8; Nehemiah 9:2 10:28; 13:3)
23. Even in heaven certain groups will not be allowed to worship together (Revelation 7:7-17; 14:1-5; 15:2-5)
24. Segregation was so strong in the O.T. that an ox and an ass could not work together (Deuteronomy 22:10).
25. Miscegenation caused disunity among God's people (Numbers 12).
26. Stock was forbidden to be bred with other kinds (Leviticus 19:19).
27. Sowing mixed seed in the same field was unlawful (Leviticus 19:19)
28. Different seeds were forbidden to be planted in vineyards (Deuteronomy 22:9)
29. Wearing garments of mixed fabrics forbidden (Deuteronomy 22:11; Leviticus 19:19)
30. Christians and certain other people of a like race are to be segregated (Matthew 18:15-17;
31. Corinthians 5:9-13; 6:15; 2 Corinthians 6:14-15; Ephesians 5:11; 2 Thessalonians 3:6-16; 1 Timothy 6:5, 2 Timothy 3:5).

CHAPTER SEVENTEEN

THE COLOR OF THE ANCIENT EGYPTIANS

Psalms 105: 23 "Israel also came into Egypt, and Jacob sojourned in the land of Ham."

It is very sad to hear the lies and to see the awful vail of half-truths that has been propagated in regard to the color of the early Egyptians. The Egypt of today is very different, both racially and geographically, than the Egypt of the days and times of Moses. During the 400 years of Israel's captivity and bondage, the ancient Egyptian's descent was of an African black people. This is very plainly seen from what the scripture says about them. They were direct descendants of Ham. Ham is the progenitor of all black tribes and people. His sons, Cush and Mizariam where the founders of Egypt.

Egypt was actually a colony of Ethiopia (Cush). Egypt was divided into two parts, there was Upper Egypt, and this was called Nubia or Northern Ethiopia. Then there was Lower Egypt, which is situated on the Mediterranean Sea, and located in the northern most part of Ethiopia. Egypt was originally called Chem, or Chemi, which means, "The land of the blacks." This is the historically documented name before it was called Egypt. When the name was changed to Egypt, it was a name derived from the name of a black king.

Interracial Marriage

Black kings started the dynastic system of dynasties in 3100 B.C. They purposed to leave markings of their presence in the land, hence, the pyramids and the Sphinx. The builders of the pyramids and of the Sphinx where black African people. Yet, for hundreds of years there has been a tremendous cover-up of these historical facts. This historical manipulation has unfortunately caused people, especially those of us in America, to view Egypt in a "distorted Hollywood" framework.

In any examination of the Sphinx, or any other artwork of Egypt, that came about during biblical times, will always readily reveal the African features of the nose, the lips and the hair. Some historians say that Napoleon actually shot off the nose of the Sphinx with a Cannon, when he saw the African features of the famous monument. So, why do I make mention of this atrocity in this book? So that you will know that the Hollywood version of Egypt is just that, the Hollywood makeover version.

CHAPTER EIGHTEEN

WHAT IS THE DEVILS PURPOSE IN HIS OPPOSITION TO INTERRACIAL MARRIAGES

Ephesian 3:11, (KJV), "According to the eternal purpose, which he purposed in Christ Jesus our Lord."

Acts 15:18, (KJV), "Known unto God are all of his works from the beginning of the world."

In order to understand the devil's purpose in the prevention of interracial marriages, one would have to better understand that God had a purpose first. The devil's purpose always comes up contrary to the purposes of God. We have previously mentioned, in this book, the purposes of God, as it pertains to race. I would like you to also view this from another perspective. God embraces the idea that He has, at His disposal, different channels through which He can express Himself, one of those channels is through racial variation.

Because of the un-limitedness of God and who He is, it behooved God to bring forth a varied makeup of mankind through which He could work. He decided their variations would be black, white, yellow, brown and red. The devil is opposed to any expression of God, and remember, man was made in God's image, which the devil hates! The devil would like for man to know and understand as little about God as possible. This allows him to distort the image of God, and also to distort what and who man is.

Jesus declared that "We, the church," are the light of the world. It is for this very reason, and absolutely imperative that we shed light on this subject. We are the ones that should truly understand this. When racism rears its ugly head in any form, it is a direct attack on the purposes of God, the wisdom of God and the very image of God. One thing I am sure that you are aware of, and that is, that the devil hates God! The main reason being, man is created in the image of God and is the object of God's affection. God loves man so much that He has even called man God out of His own mouth.

John 18:34" Jesus said is it not written in your law, I said ye are gods?"

The last thing the devil desires to see is millions of little gods moving about the world with God expressing Himself through them. These are the added channels which can developmentally manifest through the breaking down of racial lines. There is so much that God has imparted into each of us as individuals. For some, it may be the peculiarity of their racial makeup. It was never the purpose of God that we would worship racial traits but, how about in some cases He wanted an impartation and/or a diffusing of those traits into other people. To consider this is akin to the law of spiritual reproduction.

If the church is to function in that we only worship with one race of people, then by default it will only produce one kind of Christian. If you have walked in these kinds of dry, sterile, and lifeless environments, I am sure you know exactly what I mean. Everyone looks the same, acts the same, and has the same manifestation. Paul tells us in 1 Corinthians 14:26, (KJV), "How is it then, brethren? when ye come together, every one of you hath a psalm, hath a doctrine, hath a tongue, hath a revelation, hath an interpretation.

Let all things be done unto edifying." If you will notice, this is not a cookie cutter service. In this kind of service everyone has something to share. Each person has a different manifestation. This is how the kingdom should act and function, the ability for the kingdom to act and function in a very diverse way. This can only be further enhanced, by racial diversity in the house of God, as well. God in His great wisdom, imparted aspects of Himself into various races, and enhanced the ability to manifest the various aspects of what He is, by interracial marriage. He was able, if you will, to expand the bandwidth of Himself. In so doing He can express the greatness of what and who He is.

I have been amazed as I have talked with many Christians about this issue. Very often I hear the same worn out clichés parroted. What about the children? The children will suffer, they will be confused, etc. I see these reasonings as false. Children, that grow up in homes full of love and the presence of God, have an insulation that will take them through whatever they will face. At the end of the day, the fact of the matter is, is that adults have more problems with this perspective than children. We are on the verge of the greatest move of God that this world has ever seen. Some have called it the "third day move," and we are the people of the third day.

I believe that there is coming a tremendous move of God in Africa, South America, Asia and in the Muslim world. The Islamic wall is the next one to come down. This will most assuredly be a "Brown Movement," and get ready to see it come to pass.

There is no question that the face of the church has to change. For far too long the church has been in separate camps over the issue of race, which watered down the effectiveness of the church. This nation, America, has paid a great penalty over it's reluctance to address this issue. We have suffered socially, economically, and in many other ways. This is all to the delight of Satan!

PROPHETIC WORD

"Would not the Lord speak this word? Look at how this nation has lost great blessings because of the issue of race, as millions were shut-out because of the color of their skin. This has been a curse and a blight on you as a nation, saith the Lord. I seek, in this hour, to heal the rift in the spirit. I now raise up this word for you to hear and to understand that thing that I shall say at this time. If this nation will not address this issue, this nation will be likened unto Israel, a people that never saw My plan fulfilled for them. I say, hear this word, America.

I give to you the time needed, in order to correct this error. I have given you rest from war and communism. Now, I call you to look in and heal. If you will change as a nation, I will bring great change and blessing upon this nation. If you will not, I will allow this nation to be pushed aside, for I am God of all the earth and all the nations are but dust before Me.

Think not to say to yourselves, "...we are Americans, we are the great and strong." For there were many nations that were great and strong, even before you, but they no longer are in existence.

I speak a special word unto you, black Americans; I have seen the years of your suffering and your pain. The hour of your change is now and I will begin to heal all of the wounds that you suffered in America down through many decades. But I say to you, let not the enemy bring hatred into your hearts because of the things that have happened to you, as a people. Do not take on the spirit of those that have hated you. I allowed you to go through this season of pain and a time of tears; that I could make you especially sensitive to the tears of others. Let not the enemy put bitterness in your heart. It is surely the hand of God that is begun to raise up the truths of the greatness of the past, as it pertains to Africans; I did this to heal your wounded souls. But I say to you, let not this knowledge become a God to you, freely flow in the restored and new confidence that I, even the Lord, has now begun to put back into your hearts. For some of you have begun to develop the same spirit as those that did you much wrong. I say keep thy heart with all diligence for out of it are the issues of life." Saith the lord.

CHAPTER NINETEEN

INTERRACIAL MARRIAGE THE SOLUTION TO AMERICA'S RACIAL PROBLEM

Matthew 19: 5-6, (KJV), "And said, for this cause shall a man leave father and mother, and shall cleave to his wife and they twain shall be one flesh. Wherefore they are no more twain, but one flesh. What therefore God hath joined together let not man put asunder."

PROPHESY

"The Lord even thy God would say this word. I look over the face and the makeup of the nations. All nations are as dust in My hand, My plan for the nations and races of men is greater than all that you could imagine. If you will search My book, you will see My great plan for all the races of men. If you will study carefully you will begin to see. I even blend it and make a blend out of My ancient people Israel, saith the Lord. But, the devil has deceived you and has caused you to worship and fall down at the altar of the god of skin. Why would you fight and try to prevent the greatness of My plans.

I, the Lord your God, will begin to bring together your sons and daughters of every race. I will use this strategy to destroy the devil's plot that pertains to the spirit of racism, for two shall become one flesh. The white and the yellow produce the brown. The yellow and the black shall produce. The brown and the red shall produce. As this is brought forth, then I, even thy God, will end the racial problem in this land. For then shall you be sons and daughters of each other. Get ready, for it shall surely come to past, and I will do it. It shall be in the newspapers and the magazines; the world shall talk of the browning of America.

This will cause strength to flow into you, as thou shall become one flesh. I will surely do it, and I will surely bring it to pass," saith the Lord. There is, without question, a great problem in this country over the issue of race. In 1965 we had racial riots in major cities. In 1992 we again had race riots. The only difference in the two riots was that in 1992 the race riots included large numbers of other races. Most of the people arrested in the L.A. riots were Hispanic.

Looking at history, we see the Red-summer of 1914 when black World War II veterans were killed in white race riots across this country. Why? Because they had the audacity to think that after going to fight wars for this country, the U.S. A., that there would be a possibility they would then be respected, when they came back home...how wrong they were!!

We normally view race, in this country, as a black and white issue, however in Los Angeles, we began to see that it is not just black and white anymore. We have, in America, the legacy of the American Indians, not only driven off of their lands, but exterminated, as well. There is also the history of the Chinese in America. In 1918, there was the Chinese Expulsion Act. This act legitimized discrimination against the Chinese. Their plight, in this country, became so bad that the phrase, " Not a China man's chance," was coined during this period. Furthermore, there was discrimination against the Irish and the Italians in the early parts of the 20th century.

There is one significant difference that we need to take into consideration. Of the latter two groups, it was the European group that managed to overcome these problems and to steadily move forward. The question is why? The answer is simple, their sons and daughters married and intermarried with other races, until the two became one flesh. In 2012, it was discovered that the average white American is a polyglot of many different nationalities. God knew beforehand and planned it that way. This barrier has been slow to come down between blacks and whites.

The hard reality is this, as we have mentioned earlier, Two-thirds of American blacks have at least one white ancestor. So, the divide has really been breached a very long time ago, the breach occurred during slavery. So, why all the hypocrisy now? Today, we act as if this is not the fact, as we see the many shades of brown, caramel, toffee, and mocha among American blacks, and we see it with whites, because it is still apparent in some that have kinky hair and to a lesser degree, those with darker skin tones.

The solution to the racial problem is this, the sons and daughters of all Americans should be free to fall in love with whoever, whenever, wherever, and then marry, if they so choose. The Lord has dealt much with me about this. The world has a sneaking suspicion that this is the solution. The church acts as if they have no clue at all, but God will bring it to pass, anyway.

I have been greatly amazed over my conversations with Holy Ghost filled, tongue-talking Christians, as I talked to them about this issue, when I have asked the following question. "What would you do if your son or daughter wanted to marry someone of another race?" In many cases, all their faith confessions vanish. They get real 'earthy' and begin to speak the standard clichés of the world. "What about the children? The children will have problems, etc." The fact of the matter, is this; God is going to bring this to pass, despite the reticence of the church. This attitude reminds me of the attitude of Peter in Galatians 2:11-14. Paul is able to reveal Peter's racist position, as it pertains to the race issue, when confronted by the Jews. Peter was actually afraid to sit down and have dinner with the Gentiles, so he vacillated until he caved in to the prejudices of the Jewish Christians.

Galatians 2:11-13 (KJV) 11 But when Peter was come to Antioch, I withstood him to the face, because he was to be blamed. 12 For before that certain came from James, he did eat with the Gentiles: but when they were come, he withdrew and separated himself, fearing them, which were of the circumcision. 13 And the other Jews dissembled likewise with him; insomuch that Barnabas also was carried away with their dissimulation.

Paul tells us that Peter dissembled; the word dissembled is the Greek word (hupokrsis), which is the Greek word for hypocrisy. In other words, when confronted with the race issue, he,(Peter), was hypocritical. Paul said in verse 14, "... they were not walking uprightly according to the truth of the gospel." When today's Christians still will not deal with the fact that God is no respecter of persons, and that He, of one blood made all nations, leaving our sons and daughters free to marry and love anyone, then we are not walking upright, according to the gospel. This is God's solution to America's racial problem. Some people will certainly view this as a bitter pill, but I, personally, think that it is a wonderful prospect. I believe God also had this in mind when He said that the two shall become one flesh.

When people marry interracially, their offspring becomes the literal fulfillment of the two becoming one flesh. When black, white yellow and brown marry one another, their offspring becomes the fulfillment of that word. The two races now become a new race.

PROPHESY

The Lord says this word, "If you will take hold of this truth, that two shall become one flesh, just know that even though the devil has attacked and fought against this truth, I will make it manifest in this time. As the world gropes and looks for solutions, I give you this truth. Do not fight this truth, but receive it in your spirit and allow it to grow within your heart. Everything that I do, starts as a seed, but it grows, it develops, and it increases. So I, the Lord, have released this seed into this nation and it will continue to grow and develop until it fills the whole land."

We will never be one people, in this nation, until this becomes a reality. To become one people, that share a common culture and have the same thread to run through us all.

This, friend, is not always the case for black America, because our lives and our culture has never really been included in the melting pot. I am sure there are many, both black and white, that will not want to receive this truth.

I understand their concern to want to preserve the past, but we do not live in the past, we must be actively living in the here and now. We must go on. There is nothing sacred about the past, there is nothing sacred about your race, there is nothing sacred about your bloodline, or your white skin, nor your black skin, so we must stop worshiping skin and move on.

Population and demographic experts had already previously predicted that by the year 2000, the Hispanic population would become the largest minority in the U.S. What an abuse and misuse of the truth this turned out to be. Hispanic is not a racial designation. Hispanics are often many races, white, black, mulatto, Indian, etc. In many cases, Hispanics are

just people that would be classified black, if not for the fact that they speak Spanish. This is a subtle attempt to deny the browning of America. The future is brown and cocoa, caramel, off white, and brown yellow. Receive and believe and watch God solve the racial problem in this country.

CHAPTER TWENTY
A COAT OF MANY COLORS

Genesis 37:3 (KJV), "Now Israel loved Joseph more than all his children, because he was the son of his old age: and he made him a coat of many colors."

There is very deep and important truth to be seen in the coat of many colors that was placed on Joseph, by his father. This was not just an ordinary coat, given to a son by a doting father. But let us examine this scripture and we will see a spiritual mystery that will open our eyes and give us great insight. The first thing we need to see is the nature of the coat. This was, in fact, no ordinary coat, but a coat which had a very significant meaning. The coat that was given to Joseph was actually, a priestly garment and it reflected a number of things.

One thing it reflected was the fact that it was Joseph who had inherited the birthright. Another thing that this garment pointed to was Joseph's ability to understand dreams and visions. In the Old Testament we see where God began to develop the Levitical priesthood. When the garments were made, per the instructions of God, they were instructed to make the garments of many varied colors.

Exodus 28:3-5 (KJV)," And thou shalt speak unto all that are wise hearted, whom I have filled with the spirit of wisdom, that they may make Aaron's garments to consecrate him, that he may minister unto me in the priest's office. 4 And these are the garments which they shall make; a breastplate, and an ephod, and a robe, and a broidered coat, a mitre, and a girdle: and they shall make holy garments for Aaron thy brother, and his sons, that he may minister unto me in the priest's office. 5 And they shall take gold, and blue, and purple, and scarlet, and fine linen."

If you will notice in these verses, particularly in verse five, the garments that were made for Aaron were made of many colors. This was the personal design of the Holy Spirit. The priestly garments were to have multiple colors for a very specific reason. The multiple colors represented various aspects of the ministry of the Holy Spirit. We know prophetically that every color has a prophetic meaning. Also, another part of that mystery, is that each color reflected light differently when worn as they ministered before the Lord; there are aspects of physics involved. This is done, because when various colors are on our physical bodies, light is reflected in various bandwidths, which communicates certain messages in the heavens and thereby opens certain portals.

The Hebrew word **kethoneth** can be translated as 'garment', 'tunic of skin', 'worn next to the person', 'garment with long skirts and sleeves', or 'a holy linen tunic of a High Priest'. Kethoneth finds its first use in the Old Testament in the account of the 'coats of skins,' made by God for Adam and Eve, (Genesis 3:21). The King James translators could just as well have rendered this 'garments of skin' or 'robes of skins'.

The Hebrew word for skins, **Or**, has a homonym, which means, 'light'. The oral reading of the phrase, 'garments of skins', in Hebrew, conveys the meaning "garments of light."

Interracial Marriage

Priests are always connected to intercession, and intercession, in the Scriptures, is frequently connected to light.

We see this so clearly in the book of Revelation, when incense ascended upward to the throne of God, and God responded by light. Revelation 8:3-5, (KJV), 3 "And another angel came and stood at the altar, having a golden censer; and there was given unto him much incense, that he should offer it with the prayers of all saints upon the golden altar which was before the throne. 4 And the smoke of the incense, which came with the prayers of the saints, ascended up before God out of the angel's hand. 5 And the angel took the censer, and filled it with fire of the altar, and cast it into the earth: and there were voices, and thundering's, and lightning's, and an earthquake."

We also see later on, in the Old Testament, there came a point in which the priests had something on their breastplate called the Urim and Thummin. These two stones which were on the breastplate of the priests were called light and understanding. This signifies the connection of the priestly garment to light, insight, and revelation.

The significance of Joseph's priestly garment is understood even more so, as we discern the fact that the light and understanding of many bloodlines is carried in the lineage of multiracial people.

One of the ministries of the priestly order is to be spiritual porters who are the custodians over portals. Another aspect of the various colors on Joseph's garment was the fact that the Hebrew people were a multi-racial people, a composition of many different bloodlines. They were Afro-Semitic, as we have already pointed out. There are also many examples in the Scriptures of the Hebrews intermarrying other races, particularly the descendants of Cush and Ham. Joseph, himself, also typifies the experience of the current day African-American.

It was Joseph's very own brothers who sold him into slavery. Joseph, however, was given custodial responsibility over another man's house and brought wealth to that house without any personal compensation of his own. He was brought to imprisonment because of the supposed relationship with a woman, who at that time, was of what was thought to be a superior race. Many times, African-Americans are referred to as "the Joseph Company."

Figuratively speaking, in many areas, Joseph so accurately depicts the experience of the African-American. As already stated earlier in this book, today's African-American is a highly mixed personage. Joseph's coat of many colors typifies his unique ability, when in his prayer closet, to intercede from a priestly posture for the many different races that were in him as one person.

This is one of the very reasons why the devil is so fearful of interracial marriage, because he understands the priestly aspect, of the mixing of bloodlines that gives a multiracial person the ability to have legitimacy in the prayer closet when he prays, as did the intercessors and priests.

CHAPTER TWENTY-ONE

MORE SCRIPTURAL EXAMPLES OF INTERRACIAL MARRIAGE IN THE SCRIPTURES

1. Gen. 12. Sarah betrothed to Pharaoh (Egyptian).
2. Gen. 16:3-4. Abraham conceives Ishmael through Hagar (Egyptian).
3. Gen. 20. Sarah betrothed to Abimelech (Canaanite).
4. Gen. 21:21. Ishmael takes Egyptian wife.
5. Gen. 26:34. Esau takes two Hittite wives.
6. Gen. 28:9. Esau marries a daughter of Ishmael.
7. Gen. 34. Jacob's sons pretend to give their sister, Dinah, to a Canaanite prince.
8. Gen. 38. Judah takes a Canaanite wife.
9. Ex. 2:21. Moses marries Zipporah (Midianite).
10. Num. 25. Promiscuity between Hebrew men and Moabite women; also between a Hebrew man and a Midianite woman.
11. Num. 31. Hebrews allowed to retain Midianite virgins, (for wives of course), after attacking and slaughtering the Midianites.
12. Dt 21:10-14. Hebrews permitted to marry virgin captives, (of any lineage), from any future conquests outside Canaan.
13. Jud. 14. A Philistine betrothed to Samson.
14. Ruth. Ruth (Moabite) married to Boaz.

15. 2 Sam. 3:3. Maacah, (Geshurite, one of the unconquered peoples east of the Jordan), mother of Absalom, wife of David.
16. 2 Sam. 11. Uriah, (Hittite), husband of Bathsheba, (or if Bathsheba was not Hebrew then her marriage to David was interracial).
17. 1 Ki. 3:1. Solomon married to Pharaoh's daughter, (Egyptian).
18. 1 Ki. 11:1-3. Solomon had many foreign wives and concubines.
19. 1 Ki. 16:31. Ahab married to Jezebel, (Phoenician).
20. 2 Ki. 17:24. Assyrians bring in foreigners to settle in Samaria after deporting many of the Israelites. The natives eventually intermarried with the immigrants and the resulting half-breed population became the Samaritans.
21. 1 Chr. 2:16-17. Abigail, David's sister, mother of Amasa. Recorded as married to an Ishmaelite.
22. 1 Chr, 2:34. In the lineage of Judah, Sheshan's daughter given in marriage to his Egyptian servant.
23. 1 Chr. 4:18. In the lineage of Judah, Mered married to Pharaoh's daughter, (Egyptian).
24. 2 Chr. 12:13. Rehoboam's mother, wife of Solomon, an Ammonite.
25. 2 Chr. 24:25-26. Zabad and Jehozabad, conspirators against Joash for his murder of the prophet Zechariah, sons of an Ammonite woman and a Moabite woman respectively, (the inference being that the fathers were Hebrew).
26. Ezr. 9-10. widespread taking of wives from foreign nations among Hebrew men returned from exile.
27. Esther. Esther married to Ahasuerus (Persian).
28. Matt 1-5. In genealogy of Christ, Rahab, (Canaanite), married to Salmon.

29. Acts 16:1. Timothy the son of a Hebrew mother and a Greek father.
30. Acts 24:24. Felix, a Roman official, married to Drusilla.

Notes

Book Ordering Information

Other Books Written By: Chief Apostle Joseph L. Prude

Prophetic Laboratory
Office of the Dream Master
Dream Masters College Curriculum
Female Apostle
The False Bishop
Restoring Healing in The African American Church
The Creation
Ministry of the Apostle
Office of the Chief Apostle
Ministry of the Prophet
Ministry of the Prophet Level 2
The Certified Prophetic Trainer
The Highjacking of the Gospel
The Secrets of His Presence
The Mystery of Angels
The False Teaching of the Tallit
How to Interpret Any Dream
Interracial Marriage
Prophetic Proverbs
The Ministry of Fasting and Prayer

josephprude@gmail.com
Order books on amazon.com or
www.ajpministries.com

ISBN 978-1-5136-1835-7

Made in the USA
Middletown, DE
25 September 2022